W9-BAM-998

DISASTER WATCH

FLOODS

Paul Mason

A+

This edition first published in 2012 in the United States of America by Smart Apple Media.

Smart Apple Media
P.O. Box 3263
Mankato, MN, 56002

First published in 2011 by
MACMILLAN EDUCATION AUSTRALIA PTY LTD
15–19 Claremont St, South Yarra, Australia 3141

Visit our web site at www.macmillan.com.au or go directly to www.macmillanlibrary.com.au

Associated companies and representatives throughout the world.

Library of Congress Cataloging-in-Publication Data has been applied for.

Publisher: Carmel Heron
Commissioning Editor: Niki Horin
Managing Editor: Vanessa Lanaway
Editors: Philip Bryan and Tim Clarke
Proofreader: Kylie Cockle
Designer: Cristina Neri, Canary Graphic Design
Page layout: Cristina Neri, Canary Graphic Design
Photo researcher: Jes Senbergs (management: Debbie Gallagher)
Illustrator: Peter Bull Art Studio
Production Controller: Vanessa Johnson

Manufactured in China by Macmillan Production (Asia) Ltd.
Kwun Tong, Kowloon, Hong Kong
Supplier Code: CP January 2011

Acknowledgments
The publisher would like to thank the Victoria State Emergency Service for their assistance in reviewing these manuscripts.

The author and publisher are grateful to the following for permission to reproduce copyright material:

Front cover photograph: Volunteers help to evacuate trapped residents from their flooded house in Jakarta, 05 February 2007, courtesy of Getty Images/AFP.

Photographs courtesy of: Corbis/ Miao Qiunao/Xinhua Press, **18**; FairfaxPhoto/Heath Missen, **29**; Fema Photo/ Marvin Nauman, **27**; Getty Images/AFP, **12**, **16**, **19**, /Sean Gallup, **26**, /Marko Georgiev, **14**, /Dan Proud Photography, **9**; iStockPhoto/Anthony Baggett, **8**, /Ricardoazoury, **4**; Photolibrary/ Alamy/Andrew Fox, **10**, /Alamy/Ilene MacDonald , **20**; Photolibrary/Kim Kirby, **21**, / Jane Sweeney, **24**; Reuters/Petr Josek Snr, **15** Joe Skipper, **5**; SES, **11**; Shutterstock/Javarman, **22**, Caitlin Miirra, **7**; UN Photo/Logan Abassi, **28**; Wikipedia, **13**.

CONTENTS

DISASTER WORDS

When a word is printed in **bold**, look for its meaning in the "Disaster Words" box.

DISASTER WATCH

Natural disasters can destroy whole areas and kill thousands of people. The only protection from them is to go on disaster watch. This means knowing the warning signs that a disaster might be about to happen, and having a plan for what to do if one strikes.

We cannot stop natural disasters from happening, but being prepared can help reduce the harm caused by a disaster.

What Are Natural Disasters?

Natural disasters are nature's most damaging events. They include wildfires, earthquakes, extreme storms, floods, tsunamis (say *soon-ah-meez*), and volcanic eruptions.

Preparing for Natural Disasters

Preparing for natural disasters helps us to reduce their effects in three key ways, by:
- increasing our chances of survival
- making our homes as disaster-proof as possible
- reducing the long-term effect of the disaster.

FLOODS

Floods are the world's deadliest natural disasters. If you add together all the people killed by the worst volcanic eruption, earthquake, tsunami, extreme storm, and fire, it is less than half the number killed by the world's deadliest floods, in Central China in 1931.

What Is a Flood?

A flood happens when water spreads beyond its normal areas. For example, heavy rainfall may cause a river to spread beyond its banks, or a storm may drive seawater ashore. Floods turn into disasters when:

- the water has covered a large area of normally dry land
- the flood has happened very quickly, or
- the **flow** of water has been very destructive.

Preparing for Floods

There are three key ways to prepare for floods. You must know:

- the warning signs that a flood may be about to happen, and how to **react**
- the safest places to be if a flood arrives
- the challenges facing those who survive a flood.

EYEWITNESS WORDS

In 2009, Sarah Nimmo-Scott helped rescue people trapped by floods in England:

*"Last night … was dreadful. It was dark and windy, we were dealing with deep, fast-flowing, turbulent water, [but] we **evacuated** dozens of people."*

DISASTER WORDS
flow speed of movement
react act in response
evacuated helped to leave a dangerous area

Floods can affect massive areas, disrupting the everyday lives of thousands of people and sometimes causing terrible loss of life.

WHERE DO FLOODS HAPPEN?

Floods can happen almost anywhere in the world, usually in areas close to bodies of water. Two key areas are affected: places close to oceans, and places near rivers.

Floods near Oceans

In some parts of the world, flooding from the ocean regularly poses a big danger. The places most at risk are low-lying islands, such as Kiribati or the Seychelles, and low-lying coasts, such as Bangladesh's. Here, storms regularly drive ashore big waves that drench the land in seawater.

This map shows the world's biggest floods since 1991.

North America, 2005: almost 2,000 people died when Hurricane Katrina flooded New Orleans

Europe, 2010: floods and mudslides caused the deaths of at least 50 people on the Portuguese island of Madeira

Asia, 1998: the Yangtze River flooded, killing more than 3,000 people and leaving 14 million people homeless

North America

Europe

Asia

N

Africa

Key
Extreme floods

- 2002
- 2001
- 2000
- 1999
- 1998
- 1995
- 1994
- 1993
- 1991

South America

Australia

0   2,000 miles
0   2,000 km

Antarctica

Africa, 2009: floods in West Africa killed about 200 people and affected one million more

South Asia, 2008: floods hit India from July to September, causing more than 200 deaths

Australia, 2007: the Hunter River flooded, causing 11 deaths and the evacuation of thousands of people

Floods near Rivers

Floods can happen on almost any river. However, larger rivers, which carry more water, are most likely to cause floods. Areas that are particularly at risk from flooding are those near a river that:

- gathers water from a large **catchment area**
- flows out of high mountains
- has many **tributaries** flowing into it.

In each of these, the **flow** of water down the river can suddenly increase, causing floods.

Huge areas of New Orleans, United States, were flooded by Hurricane Katrina in 2005.

Hurricane Katrina

Date: August 23–30, 2005
Location: Gulf of Mexico, United States

Hurricane Katrina caused some of the most disastrous floods ever to hit the United States. Heavy rainfall swelled the rivers, which combined with seawater blown ashore by the hurricane and overcame flood defenses. Large areas of New Orleans were flooded and almost 2,000 people died.

WHAT CAUSES FLOODS?

Most floods happen either because heavy rainfall has caused a river to flood, or because the sea has broken through onto the land during an extreme storm.

Storms

As storms blow water toward shore, the sea level rises in a **storm surge**, which may spill onto the land. If there is also a **high tide**, the risk of flooding is even greater. The effects of such floods can reach far inland. For example, in 1066, high tides and a storm flooded large areas of London, England, 62 miles (100 km) from the sea.

Global Warming

The world's average temperature is increasing, in a process called global warming. As a result, sea levels have risen, and extreme storms seem to be happening more often. This means that flooding in areas near the ocean is likely to be more common in the future.

The combination of high tides and heavy rainfall can cause rivers such as the Thames in London, England, to flood.

EYEWITNESS WORDS

Anote Tong, President of the Pacific island Kiribati, said in 2006 that increased flooding meant:

"We are talking about our island states submerging in 10 years' time."

In January 2011, heavy rainfall caused deadly flash floods in Toowoomba, Queensland, Australia. The force of the flood's current lifted and flipped cars, carrying them away down the streets.

Heavy Rainfall

Heavy rainfall causes two key types of flood. The first type affects large areas, and the second can destroy anything in its path.

Low-Lying Areas

When extra water swells a river's flow too much, its banks burst. In low-lying areas, the floodwaters spread out and cover large areas of land.

Narrow River Valleys

In areas where a river follows a narrow valley, the flow of water is concentrated into a small area. The force of the river can be highly destructive, creating a very powerful, fast-moving **flash flood**.

Measuring Rainfall

Meteorologists measure rainfall using rain gauges. The simplest gauges are funnels that sit on top of two cylinders, one inside the other. The funnel feeds into the inner cylinder, which has measurements up the front. If the inner cylinder fills with water, it spills into the outer one, which is also marked.

DISASTER WORDS

flash flood flood that happens suddenly, with little or no warning

meteorologists experts in the science of weather

WHAT HAPPENS BEFORE A FLOOD?

Floods all have the same cause: too much water! However, not all floods arrive in the same way. Some floods give more warning that they are coming than others.

Extreme Weather

Ahead of the flood itself, there will be a period of extreme weather. Either a big storm hits, or there is heavy rain. However, the rain may fall hundreds of miles from the places where flooding is a risk, and the people about to be flooded may not know what is coming.

EYEWITNESS WORDS

Jonathan Oaten witnessed flooding in Prague, the Czech Republic, in 2002:

"Cars ruined, houses collapsed, the horror and sorrow on … people's faces. To have lived and seen this in a city I love is heartrending."

Saturated Ground

Floods are made worse if the ground is already **saturated**. This usually happens after a long period of rainfall. Once the ground is saturated, any extra water from a storm will cause a flood rather than being absorbed into the soil.

A combination of heavy rainfall and saturated ground causes floods.

How Quickly Do Floods Arrive?

Different types of floods arrive at different speeds.

Creeping Slowly Higher

Once rivers have burst their banks and flooded the surrounding land, the water tends to creep steadily higher. On flatter land, the water is spread over a large area, so even though the water level may rise just an inch (a few centimeters) it involves millions of quarts (liters) of water.

Flash Floods

As the name suggests, flash floods happen quickly. A great **torrent** of water can appear extremely rapidly and cause terrible destruction.

Floods Caused by a Storm

Stormwater floods can happen overnight or during the course of a day, covering huge areas.

DISASTER WORDS

torrent fast-flowing current

The 2004 Boscastle Flood

Date: August 16, 2004
Location: Cornwall, England

The 2004 Boscastle flood was one of Britain's most destructive flash floods. Extreme rainfall led river levels to rise 6 feet (2 m) in one hour. Then a 9-foot (3-m) wave, which had been held back by debris under a bridge, swept down the river into Boscastle. Many buildings were wrecked, but fortunately no one was killed.

In June 2005, 6,000 people from Lismore, Australia, had to be evacuated after a flash flood. A massive 14 inches (368 mm) of rain fell in 24 hours.

WHAT HAPPENS DURING A FLOOD?

Floods can have wide-ranging effects on infrastructure. They also pose health hazards and other risks. Once a flood has arrived, it may be around for days – or even weeks.

Damage to Infrastructure

Roads are likely to be blocked and trains will not operate. Bridges and other structures may have been flooded or weakened by the floodwaters, so they are too dangerous or unstable to use. Supplies of power and water are also likely to be disrupted.

Standing Water

Standing water is floodwater that barely moves, draining away only very slowly. This water may contain chemicals, sewage, or rotting **carcasses**. It will become a health hazard to people, animals, and plants. After flooding in Bangladesh in 2004, more than 100,000 people were affected by diseases in the water.

EYEWITNESS WORDS

In 2001, Lucius Chikuni witnessed terrible flooding in Malawi:

*"All roads to the area have been destroyed, so **relief efforts** are becoming impossible."*

When the lower levels of their house were flooded, this family in Pandeglang, Indonesia, were forced to shelter in the roof.

Flood Duration

The type of flood will affect how long it will affect the local area.

Floods from Saturated Soil

A flood that has covered large areas of land can be around for weeks. If the soil was already **saturated** before the flood, it takes a long time for all the water to drain away.

Seawater Floods

Seawater floods take a long time to drain away, too. They may even be prevented from draining away by sea defenses that were designed to keep water out.

Flash Floods

Flash floods are usually over quickly, as large amounts of water wash through and disappear.

DISASTER WORDS

saturated holding as much water as it possibly can

The 2004 Dhaka Flood

Date: September, 2004
Location: Dhaka, Bangladesh

The waist-deep waters of the 2004 Dhaka flood brought Bangladesh's capital city to a standstill. Almost every major road was blocked, and all government offices were closed. There were no trains or buses, and food markets and stores closed.

WHAT DAMAGE DO FLOODS CAUSE?

Floods cause many different kinds of damage. Violent flash floods can tear down bridges and buildings, but slowly rising floods can be even more damaging. They affect people, animals, and the natural environment.

Human Impact

Floods affect people in two key ways: by injuring and killing people, and by damaging property.

Injuring and Killing People

People often underestimate the force of flowing water, and may be swept away trying to cross floodwaters. Rising water levels can also trap people inside roof spaces. If the water does not drain away quickly, there is a risk that it will spread disease.

Damaging Property

Even structures that appear to have been only slightly affected by floodwaters may actually be badly damaged. The ground floors and basements of houses usually become waterlogged, which means that the plumbing and electrical systems need to be repaired.

EYEWITNESS WORDS

Flooding along the Thames River, London, England, in 2003, forced Caroline Spector to evacuate her house:

"We've had high tides here before and ... usually, the water just recedes. But this time, it just kept getting closer and closer to the house."

In 2005 in New Orleans, United States, people had to escape from their roofs as rising floodwaters destroyed the ground floors of their homes.

This rhinoceros was rescued from a zoo in Prague, Czech Republic, after the August 2002 flood.

Environmental Impact

Floods affect the environment, and the animals that depend on it for survival.

Environmental Damage

Floods damage croplands and the natural environment in similar ways. Trees and plants that cannot survive underwater quickly die. Over a long period, river floods can be a good thing – farmers in Egypt and Bangladesh rely on the rich soils brought by river floods. However, seawater floods can make soil too salty for plants to grow in.

Animals and Floods

Floods pose a danger to animals in three key ways:
- Animals may be drowned unless they can reach dry ground.
- With the land covered by water, it is hard for animals to find food.
- The only available drinking water may be polluted with chemicals and sewage.

DISASTER WORDS

famine severe shortage of food

The 2007 Pyongyang Floods
Date: August, 2007
Location: North Korea

After the devastating 2007 Pyongyang floods, North Korea asked the outside world for help. The floods had ruined about 20 percent of the country's corn- and rice-growing land, leading to fears of a **famine**.

FORECASTING FLOODS

Today, **meteorologists** and **geographers** work together to forecast when floods could happen. They are also able to tell what the likely effect of a flood will be, and how it will affect specific locations.

It took just one day's torrential rain for this intersection at Abidjan, Ivory Coast, to become flooded in August, 2010. Only four-wheel-drive vehicles could safely use the roads.

Storms and High Winds

Flood prediction at its most basic is very simple. If there is a big storm and high winds approaching the coast, or heavy rainfall in a concentrated area, there is a good chance of flooding. However, other factors make accurate flood prediction more complex.

Level of Soak-Away

Soak-away is the ability of the ground to absorb water. If the ground is already **saturated**, it will have poor soak-away. Ground that has been concreted over or sealed in other ways has no soak-away at all. Ground that has been cleared of vegetation, such as new farmland on hillsides, often has poor soak-away.

Tides

If an extreme storm threatens to flood an area of low-lying coast, the state of the tide has an important effect. If the strongest winds and rain, and highest storm surge, happen when there is a **high tide**, the flooding will be much worse.

DISASTER WORDS

high tide greatest height the sea normally reaches

Flood Mapping

Flood mapping is used to identify places in danger of flooding at particular water heights. It can be used for river valleys and for coastal regions. Governments use flood maps when deciding where it will be safe for people to build new homes.

Houses in this zone are unlikely to be flooded, but if a flood does come it will be extreme.

Area with 1-in-100 chance each year of flooding

Area with a 1-in-50 chance each year of flooding

Area with 1-in-10 chance each year of flooding

Houses located here are at serious risk of regular flooding.

This flood map shows a cross-section of a stretch of river. It shows which areas would be affected by various water heights, and the likelihood of a flood reaching specific heights.

MONITORING FLOODS

Once a flood threatens, there are systems in place to determine how bad it is. Experts chart how far the flood has reached, and the depth of the floodwaters.

Satellite Monitoring

Satellite images help experts to work out exactly how far the flood has reached. Over time, these images show whether earlier predictions were accurate, and whether the floodwaters are rising or falling.

3D Modeling

By combining satellite images with 3D computer models of the landscape the water has covered, it is possible for **geographers** and **meteorologists** to produce a very accurate picture of how deep the floodwaters are at specific locations. If a flood threatens a heavily populated area, the authorities may deliberately flood land farther upstream to release water from the river, or divert the water using canals or tunnels.

In China, the government sometimes floods empty areas of land to stop floods from reaching areas where lots of people live. In July 2010, floodwater was released from the Xiaolangdi Reservoir in Jiyuan.

By monitoring weather patterns using computers, it is possible to predict when and where floods are likely to strike.

Computer Prediction

Computers are used to work out when floods are likely to arrive at a particular location, and how big they are likely to be. The computers combine information on:

- the amount of rainfall
- the slope of the land, which is recorded on 3D maps
- the wind strength, which is measured using an anemometer
- the state of the tides (for coastal floods).

All these things show when the waters are likely to be highest and the flood most likely to arrive. They allow time for barriers, such as the Thames Barrier in London, England, to be closed to hold back floodwaters.

The 1931 Central China Floods

Date: July–November, 1931
Location: Central China

During the Central China floods of 1931, heavy snowmelt and rainfall flooded the Huang He, Yangtze, and Huai rivers, killing between one and four million people. It was the deadliest natural disaster ever.

BEFORE A FLOOD STRIKES

Even the best efforts of the authorities cannot prevent or divert all floods. Every year, floods cause damage around the world. So when a flood threatens, how do the authorities prepare to fight its effects?

Early-Warning Systems

Early-warning systems let people know that a flood may be coming. Various systems can be put in place:

- Telephone systems can send automatic warnings to people in the danger zone.
- TV and radio can be used to announce potential flooding.
- Alternative systems can be put in place in poorer countries. In parts of Bangladesh, everyone helps to get the word out once a warning reaches the town hall.

When it has been predicted that a flood will strike, most people will receive warning through weather reports on television.

The Cyclone Wanda Floods

Date: January 1, 1974
Location: Brisbane, Australia

The Cyclone Wanda floods were among the deadliest floods in modern Australian history. After weeks of heavy rain, Cyclone Wanda dumped huge amounts of extra water into Brisbane's rivers. The Brisbane River burst its banks: 14 people died and almost 7,000 homes were flooded.

This temporary flood barrier was used to hold back the rising floodwaters of the River Ouse in North Yorkshire, England.

Emergency Services

Police, fire, and ambulance services are put on alert, ready to help people stranded or in danger. In really disastrous floods, the defense forces might also be put on standby.

Temporary Defenses

Temporary flood defenses will be put up in areas likely to be badly affected. These defenses range from walls of sandbags to specially designed inflatable tubes or thick plastic sheeting.

Evacuation Warnings

If the authorities think that people are in severe danger from flooding, they may be told to **evacuate** their homes and move to higher ground. However, sometimes people ignore these warnings. Some of the people who died in the flooding that followed Hurricane Katrina in Louisiana, United States, had refused to be evacuated from their homes.

EYEWITNESS WORDS

In 1999, Bert Pickett witnessed flooding caused by Hurricane Floyd in North Carolina, United States:

"The water had that angry force ... it went in there like a thief and turned over everything. Turned your bed sideways. It's just devastating."

DISASTER WORDS

evacuate helped to leave a dangerous area

ARE YOU AT RISK?

Are you and your family at risk from a flood? Your local library and council offices, and the Internet, are good places to start to investigate the area where you are living or staying.

Key Questions

Measure the risk from a flood by asking key questions about an area's flood history, and whether there are preparations in place in case a flood happens. Ask the following questions about where you live, or where you are vacationing.

Are You beside a River, or on Low-Lying Ground near the Ocean?

These areas have the potential to be flooded, either by a river bursting its banks, a **flash flood**, or seawater.

Has The Area Ever Been Flooded Before?

If the area has been flooded before, check how disastrous the flood was. If it was a small flood 50 years ago, the risk is relatively low. However, three disastrous floods in the last 20 years mean there is a high risk that another might happen.

This house is safe for now, but if the waters rise it will be in danger of flooding.

Are Heavy Rainfalls or Extreme Storms Common in the Area?

Heavy rainfall and storms are key causes of floods. If these are common, and the answer to the first two questions was "Yes," then the risk of flooding goes even higher.

Do Any Nearby Rivers Have a Large Catchment Area?

A large **catchment area** would mean that the rivers can collect large amounts of rainwater, increasing the risk of flooding. The river need not be a big one: a lot of rain channeling down a small river could cause a flash flood.

What Flood-Warning Systems and Other Precautions Are There?

Check with the local council to find if any flood-prevention work has been done, and if there is a system of flood warnings or evacuation plans for the area. This will make it clear whether the authorities think there is a risk from flooding.

DISASTER WORDS
catchment area where rainfall flows into a system of rivers

Flood-Hazard Maps

Check to see if flood-hazard maps are available for your area. These may help you identify:
- which areas would be flooded by particular water levels
- the types of floods that are most likely in different areas
- how often areas are likely to be flooded.

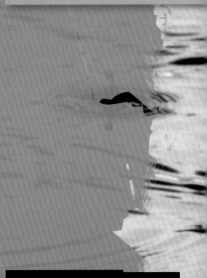

This flood-hazard map shows how likely it is that different areas will suffer flooding.

Coastal rivers – short but rapid floods

Inland rivers – long-lasting, slow-rise floods

Low flood hazard

TOP TIPS FOR REDUCING RISK

Governments and local councils do all they can to prevent flooding and reduce its effects. However, it's also important for people to take whatever action they can to keep themselves safe. So, what can you do if you live where floods are a danger?

DISASTER WORDS

evacuate leave a dangerous area

utility water, power, or telephone

flood plain the entire area over which flooding may occur

Preparing an Emergency Plan

An emergency plan is a plan detailing what everyone should do if a flood happens. Start by discussing the plan with your family. The plan should include:

- what warnings will sound if a flood threatens
- where you will all meet up
- which routes will be safest if you have to **evacuate**.

A list of emergency phone numbers will also be useful. Include your local police, fire, ambulance, emergency services, council, and **utility** companies, plus phone numbers of friends and relatives.

In some parts of the world where flooding is common, people build their houses on stilts to keep them safe from rising water.

Flood Myths

Believing some of these myths about floods could cost you your life.

1 *We recently had a 100-year flood, so I will be safe from flooding for another 100 years.*

False! The term "100-year flood" describes a flood that has a 1-in-100 chance of being equalled or exceeded in any given year. Although it is a rare event in one year, it could happen several times over a 100-year period.

2 *If my house or property was not flooded in the last flood, I do not need to worry about flooding.*

False! Some floods will cover only part of a **flood plain**, while others will cover the whole area.

3 *If my home is not on a flood plain I will be safe from floods.*

False! Flooding can occur in virtually any location, depending on weather conditions, soil type, and landscape.

Electrical cables and sockets can be sited at waist height, so that they are less likely to be damaged by floodwater.

Consider alternatives to carpets, such as removable rugs.

Make sure your home and contents are insured against flooding.

At ground level, brick and tiled walls are less likely to be damaged by flooding, and are more easily cleaned afterward.

WHAT YOU CAN DO IF A FLOOD HAPPENS

*If a flood happens and you decide to **evacuate**, do not delay. If it seems safer to stay put, take immediate action. There are plenty of things you can do to prevent disaster.*

If You Are Staying

If you are staying, use every minute to get ready for the flood. Use local radio and TV to keep up with the dangers, and:

- move vehicles, outdoor equipment, garbage, chemicals, and poisons to higher locations outdoors
- put belongings as high above ground level as possible
- get out your flood emergency kit
- make sure pets and livestock are as safe as possible
- put sandbags in toilet bowls and over all laundry and bathroom drain-holes to prevent sewage from bubbling up through them.

Residents of Hitzacker, Germany, piled up sandbags to protect against rising floodwaters in April, 2006.

Leave it too late to evacuate and you could be hitching a ride with the emergency services, like these Australian flood victims.

If You Are Evacuating

If you need, or are told, to evacuate, get moving as quickly as possible. As the waters rise, it will become increasingly difficult and dangerous to move around. Before leaving:

- pack warm clothing and valuables to take with you in waterproof bags
- pack possessions being left behind in waterproof bags, if possible
- empty refrigerators and freezers, leaving the doors open to stop them floating about
- turn off power, water, and gas, and lock up your home securely
- avoid driving across flooded roads when leaving. You do not know what is below the surface.

Flood Emergency Kit

The key ingredients are plenty of freshwater, plus food that will stay fresh for several days. Also include:
- a wind-up torch, wind-up radio, and cell phone, matches, a portable stove, cooking gear, cutlery, and can-opener
- waterproof bags for clothing and valuables
- a first-aid kit

27

AFTER A FLOOD

The danger from a flood does not end when the waters stop rising. Floodwater brings with it risks to people's health and safety. These risks may go on for days, or even weeks.

Health Risks

The biggest risk to people's health after a flood is dirty water. The water may be contaminated with **sewage** or poisonous chemicals. Drinking this water, wading through it or eating food that has been touched by it can make people sick – they may even die. Normal water supplies are likely to be contaminated by floodwater, so one of the biggest difficulties people face will be getting enough clean drinking water.

EYEWITNESS WORDS

In 2008, Midwest United States suffered terrible flooding. David Howell was in Cedar Rapids City, Iowa, United States:

"At the moment, our biggest problem is having freshwater. The rains flooded the city wells so we are all on water rationing … we have roughly a day-and-a-half's drinking water left."

Drinking water may be in short supply after a flood. In September, 2008, the United Nations sent soldiers to supply drinking water to people affected by a flood in Pakistan.

These drivers are lucky not to have been swept away: a car can float in just 2 feet (60 cm) of water.

After-the-Flood Checklist

These top tips will help you and your family to stay safe after the flood:

Do not play in or near floodwater, and never enter floodwater.

Only use gas or electrical appliances that have been checked to see if they are safe.

Never eat food that has been in floodwater.

Boil tap water until water supplies have been declared safe.

Wash, clean, and **disinfect** your home before moving back in.

Clear up **detritus** in and around your property.

Safety Issues

Being aware of the threats to people's safety during a flood could save lives. Buildings weakened by water damage could collapse, so stay out of them. Moving around is difficult unless you have a boat: floodwaters are usually very dirty, making it impossible to see what is below the surface. Electrical and gas supply systems may have been damaged. Three people were killed in 2004 in Dhaka, Bangladesh, when they were electrocuted by live electricity wires that were in contact with the water.

DISASTER WORDS

disinfect get rid of germs

detritus garbage carried by floodwaters

QUIZ: DO YOU KNOW WHAT TO DO?

Now that you have read about floods and the dangers they pose, do you feel you would have a better chance of surviving one? Test yourself using this quiz.

1 When is a flood most likely to happen?

a During a storm
b After a long period of heavy rain
c Either of the above.

2 How deep does floodwater have to be before it is unsafe to drive through?

a Up to the bottom of the car
b Up to the top of the wheel arches
c Never drive through floodwater, because you cannot know how deep it is.

3 When are flash floods most likely to happen?

a During a fireworks display
b In the middle of a lightning storm
c During or after extremely heavy rain over a small area of high ground.

4 What is the safest place to be during a flood?

a In a boat
b Up a tree
c As far above the water level as you can possibly reach.

5 What are you most likely to need once the floodwaters have stopped rising?

a A canoe for getting to the stores
b Mudguards for your bicycle
c Clean drinking water, and food that has not been touched by floodwater.

How did you do?

Mostly a or b answers: If you are planning on spending time somewhere that floods are a threat, you had better turn to page 4 and start reading again. At the moment, you are at great risk.

Mostly or all c answers: Not only would you have a good chance of survival, you might also be able to help other people during a flood.

DISASTER WORDS

flash floods floods that happen suddenly, with little or no warning

DISASTER WATCHING ON THE WEB

Being on disaster watch means being prepared. It also means knowing where to get information ahead of a disaster, knowing how disasters happen, receiving disaster warnings, and getting updates on what is happening after a disaster has struck.

World Wide Web

File   Edit   View   Help

http://www.

Find out More about Floods

Check out these web sites to find out more about floods.
- **www.howstuffworks.com**
  This site has lots of information about how floods happen, surviving a flash flood, flood prediction, and a flood quiz where you can test your knowledge (it is pretty tough, though!).
- **www.weatherwizkids.com**
  This site is particularly good at explaining how rain is formed, and also answers some unusual questions (for example, how much water is needed for a car to float away?).
- **http://news.google.com**
  Go to the search box and enter "flood," and Google News will take you to the most recent reports of serious flooding around the world.

Floods Near You

How would a flood affect your local area, and what warning might you get? To find out, contact your local government and see whether:
- they have a flood emergency plan and maps of flood zones
- they know of a web site you can look at for flood warnings.

Your local library might also be able to help you find this information.

Alternatively, these web sites might be able to steer you toward local information:
- **www.weather.gov** The US National Weather Service carries a live map showing all kinds of weather-related hazards (including flooding) in the United States.
- **www.pdc.org** has a live map of current disasters (including earthquakes, volcanoes, floods, and extreme storms), which you can click on to find out more. There is also an excellent resources section, with information about floods and other disasters.

INDEX